Early Canada
Acadians

Heather C. Hudak
Editor

Weigl
CALGARY
www.weigl.com

Published by Weigl Educational Publishers Limited
6325 10 Street SE
Calgary, Alberta, Canada
T2H 2Z9

Website: www.weigl.com
Copyright ©2007 Weigl Educational Publishers Limited

Library and Archives Canada Cataloguing in Publication Data

Acadians / editor: Heather Hudak.
(Early Canada)
Includes index.
ISBN 1-55388-236-9 (bound)
ISBN 1-55388-237-7 (pbk.)
1. Acadians--Textbooks. 2. Acadia--Textbooks. 3. Maritime
Provinces--History--To 1867--Textbooks. I. Hudak, Heather C., 1975-
II. Series: Early Canada (Calgary, Alta.)
FC2041.A2 2006   971.5004'114
C2006-902487-1

Printed in Canada
1 2 3 4 5 6 7 8 9 0 10 09 08 07 06

We acknowledge the financial support of the Government of Canada
through the Book Publishing Industry Development Program (BPIDP)
for our publishing activities.

Photograph and Text Credits
Every reasonable effort has been made to trace ownership and
to obtain permission to reprint copyright material. The publishers
would be pleased to have any errors or omissions brought to their
attention so that they may be corrected in subsequent printings.

Cover: North Wind Picture Archives; **Library and Archives
Canada:** pages 7, 43; **North Wind Picture Archives:** pages 8, 22,
34, 37.

Project Coordinator
Leia Tait

Designer
Warren Clark

All of the Internet URLs
given in the book were
valid at the time of
publication. However,
due to the dynamic nature
of the Internet, some
addresses may have
changed, or sites may
have ceased to exist since
publication. While the
author and publisher
regret any inconvenience
this may cause readers,
no responsibility for
any such changes can be
accepted by either the
author or the publisher.

Contents

Introduction

Canada is a large country with several geographic regions. The climate, land, and **resources** of these regions shaped the lives of Canada's early inhabitants. These people developed unique cultures, customs, and ways of life. The people of Acadia were distinct from the other groups who inhabited early Canada. They played an important role in developing the initial character of the country, and their influence continues to shape the nation today.

Learning about events in Canada's history can help people better understand Canada today. However, finding out what happened in the past can be a challenge. Historians must piece together history from many different sources. Often, they read historical **documents**.

Many settlers who came to Canada wrote about their experiences in journals. They also wrote letters to their families and sent reports to their **monarchs**. Some of these documents still exist. From these records,

Learning about the past is a bit like putting together a puzzle.

Acadians used straw to insulate their homes and protect the vegetables growing in their gardens. They also made straw hats and brooms.

FURTHER UNDERSTANDING

Archaeologists

Archaeologists study objects from the past called artifacts. From artifacts, archaeologists can learn the customs and traditions of the people who made and used them. They can also determine how long ago people might have lived in a certain area.

historians can learn a great deal about early people in Canada.

Historians can also learn about the past from pictures. People captured their world in paintings and sketches. Early explorers and missionaries painted plants and animals they had never seen before. They drew scenes from their daily lives and sometimes included themselves in their drawings. Historians can learn much about the activities and attitudes of early Acadians from the details in these pictures.

Historians and archaeologists also study objects from the past to learn more about people and events in Canada. Tools or cooking pots that have survived many years can reveal important facts about the daily lives of Acadians.

Learning about the past is a bit like putting together a puzzle. Pieces of information from different sources fit together to form a picture. Sometimes pieces are missing, so the picture is not complete. Then, historians must try to guess what really happened.

Historians can learn much about the Acadians from the buildings they constructed, including homes, barns, forts, and churches.

Canada's First Settlements

When explorers from Great Britain and France discovered North America, they found a land rich in resources. They filled their boats with fish and furs to carry back to their homelands. Eager to access these riches, the rulers of both countries claimed parts of this new land. To establish control over the regions they claimed, European rulers sent **colonists** to build permanent settlements. Early European settlements in North American were located in three main areas.

Great Britain built fishing settlements in what is now Newfoundland and Labrador. The British also built settlements to the south, in areas that now belong to the United States.

The French built settlements along the St. Lawrence River and around the Great Lakes. They called this large area New France. Most of the settlers who came to New France were farmers. They grew crops and raised animals for food. Some settlers earned their living from the fishing industry or the **fur trade**.

The French also built settlements on Canada's east coast in the areas now known as Nova Scotia, Prince Edward Island, New Brunswick, and the Gaspé **Peninsula**. They called this area Acadia.

FURTHER UNDERSTANDING

New France

In the early 1600s, France founded two important colonies in what is now Canada. The first **colony** wa Acadia. The second was New France. New France too in all the area around the St. Lawrence River. The colony's two major settlements were Quebec and Montreal.

Aboriginal Peoples

Aboriginal Peoples were the first people to live in No America. They believe their ancestors have always live in Canada. Scientists believe that Aboriginal Peoples are descended from ancient peoples who travelled to North America from Asia thousands of years ago. By the time Europeans arrived, many different groups liv all over North America. Each group had its own way life, its own language, its own spiritual beliefs, and its own laws.

The Quest for Fish and Furs

John Cabot was an Italian sea captain who sailed British ships. In 1497, Cabot sailed along the Grand Banks, a large body of shallow waters off the southeast coast of present-day Newfoundland and Labrador. Cabot and his crew were amazed by the amount of fish in these waters. They later reported that the cod were so numerous that they could be scooped out of the ocean in buckets.

Cabot's reports drew great interest in Europe. There, **Roman Catholic** religious beliefs forbid Europeans to eat meat on certain days. Instead, they ate a great deal of fish, especially cod. Cod was cheap and did not spoil easily. The Grand Banks were teeming with cod, and by the 1600s, fishers from all over Europe were visiting the area to fish from the abundant waters.

Fishers began sailing to the Grand Banks every summer. Some of them ventured ashore to set up temporary camps, search for food, or **preserve** their catches. There, they met Aboriginal Peoples who lived near the shore. European fishers and Aboriginal Peoples soon began to trade with one another. Fishers traded goods they brought with them from Europe, including axes, fish hooks, pots, kettles, and cloth. In return, Aboriginal Peoples supplied the Europeans with fresh meat and animal furs. When they returned home, the fishers discovered that Canadian furs, especially beaver, were easy to sell in Europe. Many European men and women desired beaver fur for hats and clothing because it was both warm and attractive.

Fishers began to trade with Aboriginal groups regularly on their summer visits to North America. Some even stopped fishing altogether to focus on trading furs. Eventually, the fur trade became a very important part of life in early Canada.

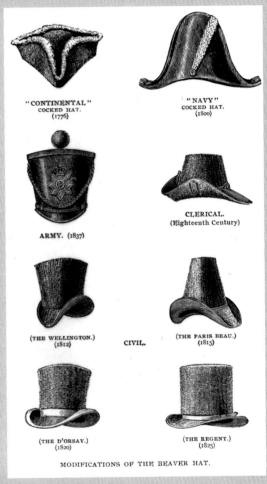

"CONTINENTAL" COCKED HAT. (1776)

"NAVY" COCKED HAT. (1800)

ARMY. (1837)

CLERICAL. (Eighteenth Century)

(THE WELLINGTON.) (1812)

CIVIL.

(THE PARIS BEAU.) (1815)

(THE D'ORSAY.) (1820)

(THE REGENT.) (1825)

MODIFICATIONS OF THE BEAVER HAT.

Beaver hats became fashionable in Europe in the 1600s. Over time, many different styles were invented.

Champlain Founds Port-Royal

When winter arrived, the newcomers were not prepared for the harsh weather.

Samuel de Champlain was an explorer from France. He travelled to present-day Canada several times in the early 1600s. His first voyage took place in 1603. As part of a trading expedition, Champlain explored the area around the Gaspé Peninsula and the St. Lawrence River. He saw that the area was ideal for settlement.

When he returned to France at the end of his expedition, Champlain shared his discoveries with the French king, Henry IV. Henry was eager to start a colony in North America. He put Pierre Du Gua Sieur de Monts in charge of an expedition to found a colony in the region Champlain had explored. In return for starting a settlement, exploring the land, and bringing religion to the Aboriginal Peoples, de Monts was granted the exclusive right to trade for furs with the Aboriginal Peoples who lived in the area.

De Monts hired Champlain as his **cartographer**, and the two became business partners. In 1604, they journeyed to North America with about 80 settlers. They sailed into the Bay of Fundy and decided to found a settlement on a small island in the mouth of the Ste. Croix River. The location was a poor choice. The island had no fresh water. When winter arrived, the newcomers were not prepared for the harsh conditions. At least 36 of the 80 settlers died of scurvy and cold.

In the spring, Champlain and the surviving settlers moved the settlement to the other side of the bay. The new settlement, named Port-Royal, was more successful. The settlers built homes and other buildings around a central courtyard. Gradually, the

Champlain was an expert mapmaker. During one voyage to early Canada, he drew a map of the St. Lawrence River and the Gaspe Peninsula.

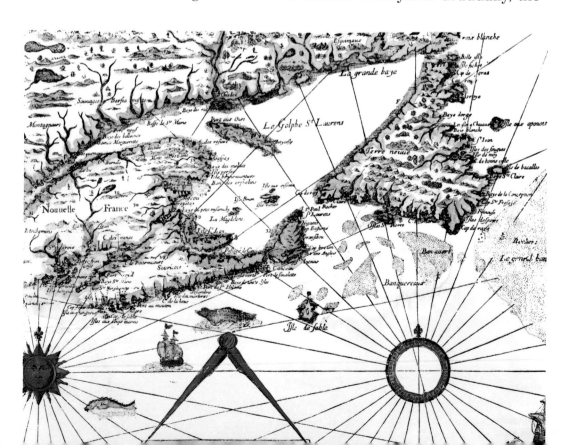

settlers adapted to the new land and climate, and the colony grew.

In 1607, the French king cancelled de Monts' fur trade monopoly. That year, de Monts and Champlain abandoned the colony and returned with the settlers to France. However, their departure did not mark the end of Port-Royal. Some of the colonists had come to think of the settlement as their home. They were determined to continue the lives they had started there. In 1610, a group of the original colonists returned to Port-Royal. They built farms along the Atlantic coast in what are now Nova Scotia, Prince Edward Island, New Brunswick, and part of the Gaspé Peninsula. Their return marked the beginning of the French colony of Acadia.

Searching for a Route to Asia

During the fifteenth century, Europeans became interested in other lands and peoples. The promise of riches made them eager to explore the unknown, where they hoped to discover new markets for trade.

European rulers in the late 1400s became particularly interested in finding a new route to Asia. They learned of exotic silks and spices available in the Far East and desired access to these luxury items.

Trade between Europe and Asia proved difficult, however. The journey between the two continents was slow and hazardous. By land, camel caravans carried goods across mountains and deserts. On the ocean, ships had to sail around the southern tip of Africa before heading to Asia, which could take months.

The desire for exotic spices, such as ginger, influenced exploration in the late 1400s.

Whoever succeeded in finding a shorter route to Asia would become very wealthy. Many monarchs and **merchants** financed the voyages of explorers in the hopes that their discoveries would lead to great wealth.

Some explorers at the time began to believe that they could reach Asia by sailing west from Europe. Those who set out across the "small" sea they believed separated Europe and Asia were surprised to discover North America blocking their way.

At first, explorers believed they had reached Asia. Once they realized the continent was a new land, they continued to search for a way through or around it. For many years, monarchs remained more interested in finding a route to Asia than exploring North America. For this reason, settlement was slow.

ACADIA: WHAT IS IN A NAME?

French settlers that came to the Atlantic region in the early 1600s called their new home *L'Acadie*, or Acadia. They called themselves Acadians. The origin of the name "Acadia" is unclear. It may have come from several words in the Algonquian language of the local Aboriginal Peoples, such as *cadie*, meaning "a piece of land," or *quoddy*, which means "a fertile place."

The name "Acadia" may also have come from the Latin word *archadia*, meaning "lands of rural peace." Arcadia was the name of a province in ancient Greece. In the fifteenth and sixteenth centuries, Europeans imagined Arcadia as a sort of earthly paradise. It was said to be a land of natural beauty, where people lived in harmony with nature. The inhabitants of Arcadia were virtuous shepherds. They happily tended their flocks and lived without suffering.

This idyllic land may have been what the first explorers imagined when they came to early Canada. Most historians believe that the name Acadia was first used by explorer Giovanni da Verrazzano. In 1524, Verrazzano explored the Atlantic coast of North America from present-day Florida to Cape Breton Island. During his voyage, Verrazzano made a map of the area he explored. On it, he named the region *Arcadie*. In his journal, Verrazzano explained that he had chosen this name for the new land because of "the beauty of its trees." Over time, other explorers and mapmakers changed the name to Acadia. They began to connect the name with various places along the Atlantic coast. By the 1620s, Acadia was the name for the Maritime region of present-day Canada.

Giovanni da Verrazzano was an Italian explorer hired by the king of France to find a route to Asia. He explored the coast of North America in 1524.

Pan, the Keeper of Arcadia

In ancient Greek **mythology**, Arcadia was home to many **supernatural** creatures, including **nymphs**, gods, and goddesses. One of the creatures that roamed the mythical Arcadia was Pan, the god of shepherds and herds.

Pan was half man and half goat. He had horns on his head, a hairy body, and hooves for feet. Pan spent his time grazing his flocks or roaming the shady woods of Arcadia, where he was born.

As the god of shepherds and flocks, it was Pan's job to guard the animals and help them multiply.

People in ancient Greece believed that Pan invented an instrument called the pan-pipes. Pan-pipes were made from pipes of increasing length strung together in a row. The player blew over the tops of the pipes to make music. The nymphs of Arcadia were said to dance to the sounds of Pan's pipes floating over land. The following myth tells the story of Pan's birth in Arcadia:

Hermes...came to Arcadia, the land of many springs and mother of flocks. There, he took his place as the ruler of Mount Kyllene. He tended curly-fleeced sheep in the service of a mortal man.

Hermes fell in love with a beautiful nymph, and the two were married. Soon, the nymph gave birth to a son. The boy was marvellous to look upon, with goat's feet and two horns. He was a noisy, happy, laughing child. But when his mother saw his horns and full beard, she was afraid. She sprang up and fled, leaving the child behind.

Hermes took his son in his arms and wrapped the boy in warm rabbit skins. He took the child to Mount Olympus, where the immortal gods lived. Hermes set his son beside Zeus, the ruler of the gods. He showed the boy to everyone present. The gods found the child appealing. He delighted all their hearts. They decided to name the goat-child Pan, meaning "everything."

French and British Settlements in Acadia

Maps do more than show where cities and towns are located. They show the distances between places. They also show which parts of the world are water and which are land.

Aboriginal Peoples drew the earliest maps of Canada. Some individuals memorized certain areas of land. When someone wanted to travel, mapmakers drew a map for them in sand or snow. Sometimes they drew maps on bark or animal hides.

Europeans began making maps of North America as soon as they arrived on the continent. Settlers who came to Acadia often relied on the knowledge of Aboriginal Peoples to help them travel around Acadia. They also relied on the Aboriginal Peoples to help them map the region. They added Acadian settlements to their maps as they were built.

Throughout the 1600s and 1700s, the French and the British competed for control of Acadia. Both nations founded important settlements throughout the area. In 1763, the English won control of all the settlements. The following map shows the locations of some of the major settlements founded in the area.

Beaubassin
- Beaubassin was one of the first major settlements founded by Acadians outside of Port-Royal.
- It was built in the early 1670s, in present-day Nova Scotia.
- Beaubassin was located in the Tantramar marshes, one of the largest salt marshes in North America.
- Beaubassin was a cattle-ranching settlement.

Grand Pré
- Grand Pré was founded in Nova Scotia in 1680.
- It was among the first settlements founded by Acadians outside of Port-Royal.
- The name Grand Pré means "Great Meadow."
- The area became an important centre of agriculture.

Halifax
- Halifax was founded in 1749 by **Colonel** Edward Cornwallis of Great Britain.
- It was built on the shores of Chebucto Bay.
- Halifax was the first government-sponsored settlement in North America.
- It was the capital of Nova Scotia and today is the largest city in the Maritimes.

Louisbourg
- Louisbourg was founded in 1713, on Île Royale.
- The fortified town was an important military **garrison**, fishing port, and centre of trade.
- The fortifications around Louisbourg were not completed until 1745.
- That same year, Louisbourg was captured by British troops, but was later returned to the French.

French and British Settlements in Acadia

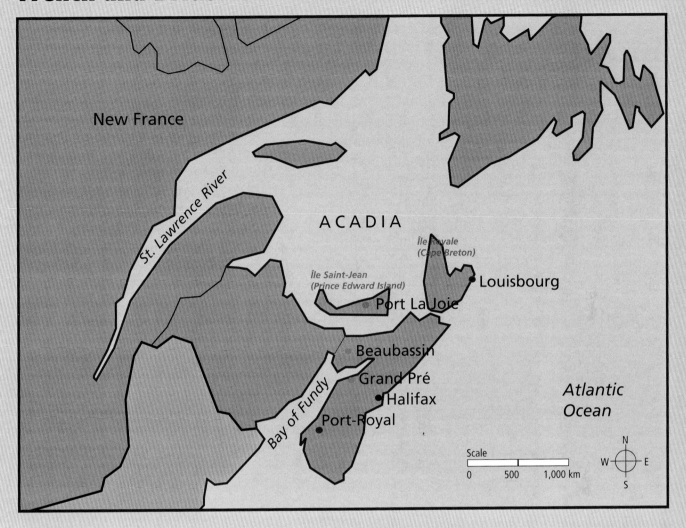

- The fortress fell to the British once again in 1758, during the Seven Years War. It remained under British rule from that time forward.
- Today, Louisbourg is a historic site. It has become the largest historical reconstruction in North America.

Port La Joie

- Port La Joie was founded in 1720, on Île Saint-Jean.
- It was located near present-day Charlottetown.
- Port La Joie was an important farming community in Acadia.
- It served as the agricultural base for Île Royale.

Port-Royal

- Port-Royal was founded in 1605, on the east coast of the Bay of Fundy.
- It was founded for France by Samuel de Champlain.
- Port-Royal was the first settlement in Acadia.
- When Port-Royal was taken over by the British, the settlement was renamed Annapolis Royal.
- Today, the Port-Royal National Historical Site is near Annapolis Royal.

A Colony of Farmers

Mi'kmaq people taught the first settlers how to hunt moose, deer, and bear.

The French settlers that came to Acadia settled along the Atlantic coast, an area rich in resources. The nearby forests provided trees for houses and firewood, and game for hunting. The ocean provided transportation and fish for food. The Acadians caught fish by driving stakes into the beach or a river bottom at low tide. The stakes created a circular fence called a weir. At high tide, the fish swam into the enclosure. As the tide receded, the fish were trapped.

Early Acadians tried to earn some money in the fur trade, but their trading posts were not successful. Instead, they turned to farming. Acadia possessed fertile soil in the marshlands along the Bay of Fundy, Chignecto Bay, and the Minas Basin. The marshlands extended far inland along the rivers. Acadians cleared the fields and grew crops. They grew grain such as wheat, oats, barley, and rye. They also grew hay to feed their dairy cattle.

Acadians soon discovered that the huge tides of the Bay of Fundy affected their farmland. Sea water often overflowed into their fields. Acadian farmers had to build

Acadians were the only settlers in North America to reclaim land from salt marshes for settlement.

FURTHER UNDERSTANDING

Dikes

Dikes are dams or banks of earth that are built to protect against flooding or to reroute and control water sources. Acadians used a combination of logs and earth covered with sod to create a bank higher than the level of the water. A gate was constructed to control the flow of water into and out of the area.

Weirs

Large traps or fences made from tree branches or wooden poles were placed across streams to catch fish. Once the fish were trapped, they could be easily speared.

dikes to reclaim land and keep water out of their crops.

The Acadians' diet consisted of pea soup, bread or porridge, salted beef and pork, sheep and fowl, maple syrup, and fish and game. They grew their own herbs and vegetables such as peas, potatoes, turnips, carrots, and beans. They used milk from the cattle to make cream, butter, and cheese. Men and women chewed spruce gum, which helped their digestion and cleaned their teeth. The Acadians also planted fruit trees.

Mi'kmaq people taught the first settlers how to hunt moose, deer, and bear. They also showed the Acadians how to trap smaller animals, such as rabbits. The Mi'kmaq showed the settlers which wild plants and berries were safe to eat.

For goods they could not grow or manufacture themselves, Acadians traded illegally with British settlers who lived to the south in what is now the United States. They made much of their clothing from flax cloth they bought from the British. Acadians also wove some cloth themselves. They wore flat shoes they made from sealskin and moose hides. When ships came from France, Acadians bought goods from French merchants.

Life for the early Acadians was hard work. While life was difficult, however, it was also very rewarding.

Acadians kept sheep and spun their fleece into wool to make warm clothes.

The Struggle Begins

When the French settled Acadia, the British were upset. France argued that explorer Jacques Cartier had claimed Acadia for France in 1534. The British argued that John Cabot had claimed the entire Maritime region for Great Britain when he visited what is now Newfoundland and Labrador in 1497. British settlers near Acadia feared that the French would want to start expanding the area under their control. If the Acadians spread south along the Atlantic coast, British expansion would then be threatened.

Acadia was very desirable to both France and Great Britain.

The country that controlled Acadia would have access to the Grand Banks, which were the best fishing grounds in North America. It would also control the St. Lawrence River, which provided access to the interior of the continent.

In 1613, authorities in the British colonies sent a raiding party north along the Atlantic coast. The group was led by Captain Samuel Argall. His orders were to destroy all French trading posts on lands claimed by the British, including Acadia.

Argall's raiders destroyed a number of small settlements along

> Acadia and the surrounding area were very desirable to both France and Great Britain.

In spring and summer, fields of sunflowers bloom in present-day Nova Scotia, an area that was once part of Acadia.

the coast. When they arrived at Port-Royal, the raiders stripped the fort, killed the animals, set the buildings on fire, and destroyed the fields and crops. Argall and his raiders chased away most of the Acadian settlers.

Port-Royal remined vacant until 1621. That year, the British king, James I, granted the lands of Acadia to Sir William Alexander. Alexander renamed the colony Nova Scotia, or "New Scotland." A few years later, Alexander's son brought a group of British settlers to Port-Royal, which they renamed Annapolis Royal. Another group built a small colony in present-day Cape Breton.

British settlements in Acadia were unsuccessful. By 1632, the **Treaty** of Saint-Germain returned control of Acadia to the French. British settlers in the area returned to Europe, and new French settlers were brought to Acadia. The French worked hard to rebuild Acadia. By 1650, their farms were prospering, and most families had adequate food and clothing.

Sir William Alexander never visited Nova Scotia, but he did give the colony its name, flag, and coat of arms.

FURTHER UNDERSTANDING

Treaty of Saint-Germain

In the years leading up to the Treaty of Saint-Germain, the British in North America captured a number of important French settlements, including Port-Royal in Acadia and Quebec, the capital of New France. With the signing of the treaty in March, 1632, control of these areas was returned to France.

The Growth of Acadia

During the colony's early years, Port-Royal remained the centre of Acadian life. By the 1670s, some Acadians began leaving Port-Royal to found other settlements. The most important of these new settlements were Beaubassin and Grand Pré in present-day Nova Scotia.

Beaubassin was founded on one of the largest salt marshes in North America. The Acadians built dikes to drain the land of salt water, and reclaimed the fields for agriculture. They also raised cattle at the settlement.

Grand Pré, which means "Great Meadow," was named for the enormous, fertile marshlands that Acadians discovered in the area. Grand Pré quickly became an important farming centre as it supplied both the British and French colonies in the area with agricultural products.

The availability of rich farmland and the absence of a strong colonial government meant that the Acadians who funded these new settlements were free to live on as much land as they pleased. They enjoyed their independence and took advantage of their opportunities to trade with both the French and the British.

Acadians that left Port-Royal helped each other build homes and farms at the new settlements.

Missionaries in Acadia

Beginning in the 1600s, the Roman Catholic church in France sent **missionaries** to early Canada. Missionaries built religious settlements among the Aboriginal Peoples of Acadia. They wanted to teach the Catholic religion to Aboriginal Peoples. Missionaries also provided religious services to early European settlers in Acadia.

The first French missionary to come to Canada was a priest named Father Abbé Jessé Flèché. In 1610, Flèché journeyed to Port-Royal with some fur traders. He stayed at the settlement for one year. While he was there, Flèché **baptized** a Mi'kmaq chief named Membertou, along with 20 members of Membertou's community.

In 1611, two **Jesuit** priests, Father Pierre Biard and Father Enemond Masse, arrived at Port-Royal. They learned the Mi'kmaq language in order to teach the Catholic religion to the Mi'kmaq people there.

Many other missionaries soon followed. They built more missions in Acadia, along the St. Lawrence River, and among the Huron people near the Great Lakes. In 1675, another Catholic missionary named Father Chrestien Le Clercq set up a mission among the Mi'kmaq of the Gaspé Peninsula. He was the first European to notice that the Mi'kmaq used a form of writing. Le Clercq helped the Mi'kmaq develop their system of writing so they could write down the religious ideas he taught them.

Jean-Baptiste de La Croix de Chevrières de Saint-Vallier was one of the first officials of the Catholic church to come to early Canada. He encouraged missionary work in Acadia.

INTERACTING WITH THE MI'KMAQ

The Mi'kmaq taught the Acadians how to use canoes, toboggans, and snowshoes. They also acted as guides when the Acadians needed to explore or travel. The Mi'kmaq showed the settlers how to hunt and where to fish. They showed Acadians which plants were safe to eat and which could be used to make medicine.

At first, when there were few Europeans in Acadia, the Mi'kmaq continued to hunt and fish as they wished. They were able to maintain their traditional way of life while co-operating with French settlers who moved to the area. When the **fur trade** began, the Mi'kmaq acted as middlemen between the French traders and other Aboriginal groups in the area.

As the number of Acadian settlers grew, however, the Mi'kmaq began to face serious problems. Settlers from Europe brought new diseases with them, such as smallpox, whooping cough, tuberculosis, chicken pox, and scarlet fever. The Mi'kmaq had never been exposed to these diseases before. Their bodies had not built up any resistance to them, so even measles could be fatal. Shortly after Europeans came to settle in North America, thousands of Aboriginal Peoples, including many Mi'kmaq, died as a result of European diseases.

When British settlers came to Nova Scotia, they moved onto land where the Mi'kmaq lived. The settlers cleared forests and often built farms near the best fishing areas, where the Mi'kmaq had their summer camps.

These changes seriously affected the Mi'kmaq way of life. They could not hunt and fish freely, as they had done before. To make a living, some began to make and sell crafts, such as birchbark baskets. Others went to work for the settlers. Some joined the fishers off the coast. Others helped the

> The Mi'kmaq had never been exposed to European diseases before.

The Mi'kmaq taught the Acadians how to make and use snowshoes, one of the few ways to travel in winter.

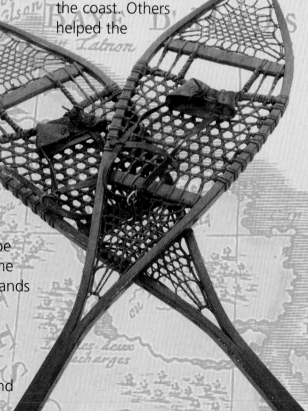

Europeans get lumber from the forests. Still others worked as guides for the settlers.

The Mi'kmaq spent less time hunting, fishing, and making things for themselves. They came to rely upon the fur traders for most of their clothes and tools, and some of their food, since game animals were reduced by European hunting.

When European fur traders deserted their fur trading posts in the Maritime region for more profitable beaver lands to the north and west, the Mi'kmaq had to find new ways to feed and clothe themselves without regular European trade. Many moved away from their traditional lands near the coast, and into the interior. There, they tried to return to their traditional life of hunting and trapping, but they continued to struggle.

Mi'kmaq and European Views

Mi'kmaq peoples and Europeans often had different points of view. The Europeans thought that they could improve the life of the Aboriginal Peoples because the Mi'kmaq wore few clothes and had no firearms or metal tools.

However, most Europeans could not understand the Mi'kmaq language, and the missionaries were unfamiliar with Mi'kmaq beliefs.

The Mi'kmaq thought that Europeans were weak. They noticed that the Europeans were unable to canoe or snowshoe very far before becoming exhausted. Their bodies and faces were also covered with "ugly" masses of hair. The Mi'kmaq also saw that the Europeans had much to learn about living off the land.

For the most part, the Mi'kmaq and the Europeans lived together in peace. They each had something other wanted, such as furs or manufactured goods. The groups continued to co-operate even after European actions began to negatively affect the Mi'kmaq way of life.

The Mi'kmaq lived in wigwams. Wigwams were light, portable structures made of bark or animal hide over wooden poles.

Disputes in North America

In its first 100 years, Acadia changed hands nine times.

Life was not peaceful for the Acadians. For much of the 1600s and 1700s, Britain and France were at war in Europe. These conflicts frequently spread to North America. The two countries competed fiercely for control of the land, resources, and colonies on the continent. British and French settlers fought one another as they reacted to the wars taking place in Europe.

Acadia played a central role in French and British conflicts over North America. A British prime minister once declared that he would rather lose his right arm than surrender the fishing grounds in Acadia. A French politician said that he would prefer to be stoned in the streets than lose the fisheries.

Often during this time, wars in Europe decided who controlled Acadia. In its first 100 years, Acadia changed hands nine times. The Acadians tried to carry on their day-to-day lives despite this

The French and British did not only fight over Acadia. In 1629, the British captured Quebec and gained control of New France. The colony was restored to the French a few years later.

turmoil. They did not want to fight for either the French or the British. They wished to be left alone, but often could not escape the constant conflict.

In 1690, Captain Sir William Phips led an expedition to Acadia from the British colonies in the present-day United States. He captured and **looted** Port-Royal, but was driven away. However, the attack marked the beginning of another conflict for Acadia between the French and British.

By 1696, the conflict continued. That year, a French soldier and adventurer, Pierre le Moyne d'Iberville, helped drive the British from the Bay of Fundy fishing grounds and led campaigns that destroyed British settlements and trading posts in what is now Newfoundland and Labrador. The struggle finally ended in 1697, when France regained control of Acadia. Peace reigned for the next four years.

Pierre le Moyne d'Iberville was a French soldier and adventurer. In 1697, he led the crew of his ship, the *Pélican*, against three British warships in Hudson Bay, defeating them all.

FURTHER UNDERSTANDING

French Raids

Battles between French and British were often brutal. In 1689, Pierre le Moyne d'Iberville took part in a vicious attack on a British village in what is now the United States, killing 60 settlers. In 1696 and 1697, d'Iberville was in charge of removing the British from what is now Newfoundland and Labrador. The French soldiers and their Aboriginal allies struck unexpectedly in winter. Since the British had only guarded themselves against sea attacks, d'Iberville was able to destroy about 36 settlements in six months. The French killed or captured hundreds of British settlers and added a vast amount of territory to the French colony.

The British Take Control

In 1701, another war broke out in Europe that would have important consequences for Acadia. The **War of Spanish Succession** was a power struggle involving many of the countries in Europe. France and Great Britain were on opposing sides of this conflict, and war soon spread to the colonies, where it was known as Queen Anne's War.

Raids began between Acadia and the British colonies. At first, the Acadians dominated the conflict, destroying a British fishing colony in what is now Newfoundland and Labrador, and capturing nearby St. John's.

However, in 1710, the tide turned when British forces captured Port-Royal and gained control of Acadia. The war finally ended in 1713, and France and Great Britain signed the Treaty of Utrecht. The treaty divided Acadia between France and Great Britain. The French kept present-day New Brunswick, the islands of Île Saint-Jean (present-day Prince Edward Island), and Île Royale (now called Cape Breton Island). They also maintained fishing rights off the north shore of Newfoundland and Labrador. In return, the French gave up their claims to Newfoundland and Labrador and Hudson Bay, and the British took the area they called Nova Scotia. Most of what had been Acadia was now controlled by the British.

Acadians in Nova Scotia

When they took control of Acadia, the British had to decide what to do with the nearly 2,500 French-speaking Acadian farmers and fishers living there. The British were **Protestant**, and they did not trust the Roman Catholic Acadians, who spoke French and listened to French-born priests. To solve their dilemma, the British gave the Acadians the option of leaving the area or remaining in Nova Scotia and becoming British citizens.

Most people decided to stay in Acadia. The British told the Acadians that to stay, they had to swear an oath of allegiance to Great Britain. The Acadians did not want to swear such an oath. They were concerned that if they did, they might be called upon to fight against France or their Aboriginal **allies**, the

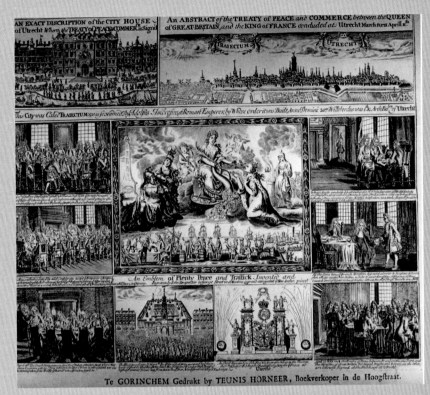

When the Treaty of Utrecht was signed, pamphlets summarizing the event in pictures were distributed throughout Europe.

Mi'kmaq, if there were another war.

Instead, the Acadians told the British authorities that they would agree to remain **neutral** in any future conflicts. Though the British did not like it, they accepted this arrangement for the time being.

FURTHER UNDERSTANDING

Oath of Allegiance

An oath of allegiance is a promise to be loyal to a particular leader or country. Such a pledge is usually signed, but can also be made verbally. A person can be punished by law for breaking a legal oath. The Acadian oath required a commitment to Great Britain, its monarchy, and its causes.

The Acadians at Île Saint-Jean

King Louis XV was anxious to bring the Acadians back under French rule.

King Louis XV of France was anxious to bring the Acadians back under French rule. He tried to convince them to migrate to areas of Acadia still held by France—Île Royale and Île Saint-Jean. However, little could convince the Acadians to leave the fertile farmland in Nova Scotia.

Despite the Acadians' poor response, Louis XV remained determined to develop settlements in the areas of Acadia that remained under French rule. Since agricultural land on Île Royale was poor, the king encouraged settlement on the fertile lands of Île Saint-Jean. In April 1720, he sent about 250 French colonists to the island.

Four months later, the ships sailed into Port la Joie, near present-day Charlottetown.

Over the next few years, the settlers built several colonies along the coast. Port la Joie became the capital of the island. A garrison of 30 poorly equipped men guarded the entrance to the harbour. Unfortunately for residents of Île St-Jean, Louis XV was not particularly interested in the settlement. Instead, he had set his sights on building a military base on nearby Île Royale. As a result, Île Saint-Jean was initially colonized only to grow food for the soldiers stationed at Île Royale.

Île Saint-Jean was largely ignored by the French until the British took control of most of Acadia.

A Letter From Marie Jeanne

Personal letters can be a good source of information for historians. The following is an imaginary letter that could have been sent from an Acadian girl to a cousin in France.

15 December 1752
Tracadie Harbour
Ile St-Jean

Dear Marguerite,

Please forgive my mistakes. We do not have schools here and my brothers and I are the only children who can read and write. We go twice a week to a neighbour for lessons unless we are needed at home.

It has been snowing all day today. Papa and my brothers did not go out except to bring in firewood and look after the cows and pigs. Papa spent the day sitting beside the fire, mending furniture and smoking his pipe. Mama and I were much busier. I helped her look after the younger children, and we also carded and spun much of the wool from our sheep. We can get linen from the new settlement on Île Royale, but wool clothing is warmer, and it does not cost anything because we make it ourselves.

Last year, our neighbours set fire to their land so they would not have to clear it. When the fire spread to our wheat field, we lost the entire crop. This year, the mice are threatening to eat all our oats.

Papa says that in the spring we may get a horse. We also hope to have piglets and calves to trade.

The nearest priest is in Port la Joie, a day's journey from here. We only go to church on important religious days. I will finish this letter now and hope it gets to you early in the new year.

Your good friend,
Marie Jeanne

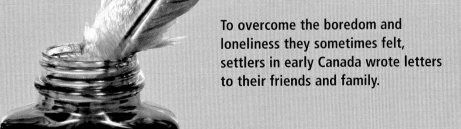

To overcome the boredom and loneliness they sometimes felt, settlers in early Canada wrote letters to their friends and family.

The French Fortify Île Royale

British and French settlers in North America found many reasons to fight each other.

To protect the remaining French colonies and guard the mouth of the St. Lawrence River, Louis XV decided to build a fortified town on Île Royale. Louisbourg, as the town was called, was, in essence, a massive military fortress. The fortifications took 25 years to complete. Instead of an agricultural centre, like most other Acadian settlements, Louisbourg was built as a military garrison, a fishing post, and a centre for trade.

In 1744, the War of Austrian Succession broke out in Europe. Once again, the war embroiled most of Europe and spread to the colonies. In North America, the conflict was known as King George's War.

Even though the war was triggered by events in Europe, French and British settlers in North America found many reasons to fight each other. Both sides wanted control of the fur trade and Atlantic fishing rights. They both also wanted to expand their settlements westward. The French wanted to get Acadia back as well.

In 1744, a French force attempted to recover Acadian lands in Nova Scotia. The force managed to seize some territories, but did not succeed in retaking Port-Royal. The British fought back, and in the following year, an untrained British force captured the fortress of Louisbourg on Île Royale. The Acadian settlers there were forced to return to France.

After Louisbourg was captured, the war continued in Europe

The highest elevations in the Maritimes are found in the highlands of present-day Cape Breton Island, formerly Île Royale.

and North America until 1748. Although the British captured Louisbourg, they lost territory in other parts of the world. At the peace talks in 1748, Great Britain traded Louisbourg back to France in return for part of India. North America returned to its status of 1713, as outlined in the Treaty of Utrecht.

Halifax–The British Answer to Louisbourg

After King George's War, British settlers in North America were unhappy that the French had regained Louisbourg. The fortress had often been used as a base from which the French launched raids on British colonies. In order to protect their settlements from raids and to take advantage of the rich cod fishing in the area, the government of Great Britain financed a new settlement in Nova Scotia.

In 1749, Colonel Edward Cornwallis set out from Great Britain with 2,500 British settlers. The group made its way to Chebucto Bay, Nova Scotia. There, they founded a settlement called Chebucto. They later changed the name to Halifax.

Halifax was the first government-sponsored settlement in North America. Like Louisbourg, it was a fortified town. Within a year,

5,000 British, Swiss, and German settlers had settled in the colony. They built a governor's home, a church, wharves, fortifications, and houses.

The Citadel is a well-known landmark in Halifax. The massive, star-shaped fort was built to guard the city against attacks on land and from the nearby harbour.

FURTHER UNDERSTANDING

King George's War

Named after King George II of Great Britain, King George's War was the North American phase of the the War of Austrian Succession in Europe. It began after the unsuccessful French attempt to recapture Acadian lands in Nova Scotia.

LOUISBOURG: ACADIA'S FORTRESS

In 1713, 150 settlers landed at English Harbour on Île Royale. Most of the group were young, unmarried men who were sent to the island to found a new settlement for France. The settlers quickly began work on a fortified town, which they called Louisbourg. It would take almost three decades to complete all of the fortifications. Even before it was finished in 1745, Louisbourg had become the centre of French power in North America.

During its construction, Louisbourg flourished. The town grew into an important fishing and trading port, and was named the capital of Île Royale. Settlers came to Louisbourg from all over Europe and North America. By 1740, nearly 2,000 settlers called Louisbourg home. That number had doubled to 4,000 by 1750. At the time, it was one of the largest populations in North America. This diverse group of colonists were occupied as government officials, professionals, merchants, missionaries, tradesmen, fishermen, servants, and slaves.

Although Louisbourg grew into a prosperous port, the fortress was first and foremost a military base. French troops guarded the post year-round. Louisbourg was protected by stone walls that were up to 3 metres thick and 9 metres high in some places. These walls were topped with cannons that pointed out to sea and were surrounded by a steep ditch for additional protection.

The fortress was built in an ice-free harbour, which the French believed could be easily defended. It was surrounded by water on three sides, and the only access from land was

Louisbourg was a strategic fortress built to defend all of the French colonies in early Canada.

across swampy ground. When it was finally completed, Louisbourg appeared as if it would stand forever.

The strength of Louisbourg was tested almost immediately after the fortification was completed in 1745. That June, following a declaration of war between Great Britain and France, British troops attacked the fortress. Their assault was aggressive. Within 46 days of the attack, Louisbourg was lost. 4,000 untrained British colonists had captured the seemingly impenetrable fortress.

Louisbourg had, in fact, several weaknesses. Some of the weaknesses were related to location. Others were related to the fortress's construction and the condition of its troops. All contributed to the fortress' capture by the British.

Louisbourg's Weaknesses and Their Consequences in Battle

WEAKNESSES	CONSEQUENCES
Louisbourg was situated in the midst of many hills, some of which were dangerously close to the fortifications.	The hills provided enemies with a vantage point to set up siege batteries and shoot cannon balls into the centre of the town.
Many coves lined the coast near the fortress.	Enemy troops could land in the coves and prepare for an attack without being seen.
Wall cannons faced out to sea but could not be turned once attackers moved onto land.	The British dragged their own cannons over land, where they easily attacked the fortress, out of reach of the French cannons.
Louisbourg was poorly constructed.	Although the fortress had thick stone walls, the damp climate prevented the mortar from settling properly, leaving the walls weak and crumbling.
Living conditions at the fortress were harsh. The troops were poorly paid and faced shortages of food and equipment.	Morale was very low among the troops at Louisbourg. Hungry, with cannons falling around them and the fortress walls crumbling, the French troops surrendered.

The British Demand Loyalty

As more British settlers moved to Nova Scotia, the Acadian presence there became a problem.

In 1749, the British moved the capital of Nova Scotia from Annapolis Royal to Halifax. The new capital had better access to fishing waters and trade routes, and was also far away from the Acadian settlements. The British government hoped that this would help attract more settlers to Nova Scotia.

The move was successful. More settlers began arriving in Halifax. They also began setting up forts and small communities throughout Nova Scotia. The settlers founded many new communities along the coast. Although most of the newcomers came from Great Britain, a significant number also came from areas of Germany that had links to Great Britain.

As more British settlers moved to Nova Scotia, they became more aware of the Acadian presence in the settlement. By the 1750s, British merchants in Halifax were complaining that the Acadians who lived in Nova Scotia were sending their produce to Louisbourg instead of Halifax. The new British settlers were

Acadian settlements along the Atlantic coast had access to fertile farmlands and the best fishing grounds.

also unhappy that the best lands in Nova Scotia were already occupied by Acadians.

As well, the British continued to distrust the Acadians. Five times since 1713, the British governors of Nova Scotia had asked the Acadians to swear an oath of loyalty to Great Britain. Each time, the Acadians had refused. They did not want to be forced to fight in the ongoing conflicts between France and Great Britain. They did not consider themselves French or British. They were Acadian. Rather than swearing loyalty to either country, the Acadians continued to pledge their neutrality in times of war. However, because the Acadians spoke French, were Roman Catholic, and followed the teachings of their priests from France, the British believed the Acadians were loyal to France.

By 1755, the Acadian promise to remain neutral was not enough for the British. France and Great Britain were again on the verge of war. The British governor of Nova Scotia, Charles Lawrence, decided to take drastic action. He ordered the Acadians to sign an oath of allegiance to Great Britain or else leave the colony.

FIRST-HAND ACCOUNT

Paul Mascarene, a British soldier and later governor of Annapolis Royal, spent a great deal of time in Nova Scotia settling disputes among the Acadians. Although sympathetic to their plight, in 1720, Mascarene became one of the first colonial officials to argue that the Acadians should be forced to pledge their loyalty to Great Britain or else leave Nova Scotia:

"The reasons for not admitting these Inhabitants are many and strong, and naturally deriving from the little dependence on their allegiance...It would therefore be necessary for the interest of Great Britain, and in order to reap the benefit that will accrue from the acquisition of this country, not to delay any longer the settling of it, but to go about it in good earnest. It is humbly proposed that the French Inhabitants may not be tolerated any longer in their non-allegiance, but may have the test put to them without granting them any further delay, for which it is requisite a sufficient force be allowed to make them comply with the terms prescribed them, which force ought to be at least six hundred men to be divided to several parts already inhabited by the French and the Aboriginal Peoples, and might be at the same time a cover to the British Inhabitants who would come to settle in the room of the French. For an encouragement, to those new Inhabitants should be given free transportation, free grants of land, and some stock of Cattle out of what such of the French who would rather choose to withdraw than take oaths, might be hindered to destroy or carry away."

Deportation of the Acadians

Acadians were divided into small groups and sent to British colonies along the east coast.

When Governor Lawrence made his demands in 1755, the Acadians once again refused to take an oath of allegiance to Great Britain unless it included a condition that they would not have to fight against the French in the future. The British refused to accept this condition.

On July 31, 1755, Lawrence ordered the Acadians to be **deported** from Nova Scotia. British soldiers rounded up thousands of Acadian settlers, herded them onto ships, and sent them away.

To prevent them from moving to nearby New France, most Acadians were divided into small groups and sent to British colonies along the east coast of North America. This policy resulted in the separation of families and friends.

Some Acadians went to French territories in the West Indies or what is now the state of Louisiana in the United States. A few Acadians fled to New France. Others escaped to the forests to join their Aboriginal allies in attacks against the British. Still others went to France.

The deportations lasted until 1762 and uprooted about 8,000 of the 10,000 Acadians who lived in Nova Scotia. To ensure that they would not return, British soldiers destroyed the Acadians' crops and set fire to their homes and other buildings.

At Grand Pré, men and boys were summoned to the church to hear the order of deportation. They were then held prisoner until British ships arrived to deport them.

The deportation of the Acadians marked a turning point in the history of the region. The British benefitted from the Acadians' hard work settling the area. After the removal of the Acadians, many British settlers from Great Britain and Ireland moved to Nova Scotia and started settlements along the coast. About 8,000 settlers from the present-day United States also settled on Acadian lands. From this time on, the Maritime colonies were largely populated by English-speaking Protestants.

Evangeline and Gabriel

In 1847, American poet Henry Wadsworth Longfellow wrote a poem about the departure of two Acadians, Evangeline and Gabriel, at the Grand Pré deportation in 1755. The following is part of his well-known poem.

Evangeline is a symbol of pride and hope for many Acadians.

There disorder prevailed,
andthe tumult and stir
of embarking.

Busily plied the freighted boats;
and in the confusion
Wives were torn from their
husbands, and mothers,

too late, saw their
childrenLeft on the land,
extending their arms,
with wildest entreaties:So
unto separate ships were
Basil and Gabriel carried,

While in despair on the shore
    Evangeline stood with
    her father.

    Half the task was not
    done when the sun
    went down, and
    the twilight

    Deepened and
    darkened around; and
    in haste

    there fluent ocean
    Fled away from the
    shore, and left the
    line of the sandbeach

    Covered with waifs of
    the tide, with kelp
and the slippery
sea-weed.

    Farther back in the
midst of the household goods
and the wagons,

Like to a gipsy camp, or a
leaguer after a battle,

All escape cut off by the sea,
and the sentinels near them,

Lay encamped for the night the
houseless Acadian farmers.
Back to its nethermost caves
retreated the bellowing ocean,

Dragging adown the beach the
rattling pebbles, and leaving

Inland and far up the shore the
stranded boats of the sailors.

Then, as the night descended,
the herds returned from
their pastures;

Sweet was the moist still air
with the odour of milk from
their udders;

Lowing they waited, and long,
at the well-known bars of the
farmyard,—

Waited and looked in vain for
the voice and the hand of
the milkmaid.

Silence reigned in the
streets; from the church
no Angelus sounded,

Rose no smoke from the roofs,
and gleamed no lights from
the windows.

People with Different Ideas

The British would not accept Acadian neutrality.

British soldiers in Nova Scotia had the unpleasant task of rounding up the Acadian settlers and burning their homes and crops.

The Acadians thought of themselves as independent. They did not want to choose sides in wars between France and Great Britain, or fight against either country. They also did not want to leave their homes in Acadia, where they had been settled for almost 150 years.

The British would not accept Acadian neutrality. They believed that if the Acadians would not fight the French, they must be enemies of Great Britain. They wanted the Acadians to leave. This is how each of these groups may have described their views.

A British Army Officer

When I attacked a French fort near Nova Scotia recently, my men found some Acadians fighting beside the French forces.

If they fought there, they might fight for the French at their large forts along the St. Lawrence River. There are so many of them, they would easily win.

I have asked the Acadians in Nova Scotia to swear an oath of loyalty to our king, George II, but they refuse. So I have ordered that they be forced to leave this settlement. They must move somewhere else, so they will

no longer be a threat to our settlement. We have tried to keep Acadian families together, so as not to cause any hardship.

An Acadian farmer

The British have forced my family and me to leave our farm. My family has lived in Acadia for more than 100 years. We have done nothing to deserve such treatment.

I never fought against the British. I just wanted to live in peace on my land. I refuse to swear an oath of loyalty because, if I did, they might put me in the army. Then I might have to fight against the French.

The British made me move to a place where most people speak English instead of French. I was separated from my wife and children when I was loaded onto a boat. I do not know what has become of them.

Until the day I die, I will never forget what the British did. I will always remember.

Acadian women watched while their husbands were sent away on the first deportation ships. Women and children were rounded up later and sent to different locations.

The Fall of Acadia

In 1756, shortly after the deportation of the Acadians, the Seven Years' War began in Europe. It quickly spread to the colonies. In North America, the Seven Years' War became a major battle between the British and the French for control of North America. In this struggle, the two countries fought for three key areas—the Ohio River Valley, Quebec, and Louisbourg.

In the first few years of the war, the French forces in North America held their own against the British everywhere but in Île Royale and Île Saint-Jean—what remained of Acadia. In 1758, the British attacked Louisbourg.

Without a strong navy to patrol the sea beyond its walls, the fortress was impossible to defend. Attacking with 16,000 troops supported by 150 ships, the British army captured Louisbourg in seven weeks. Determined that the settlement would never again become a fortified French base, the British demolished the fortress walls.

The same year, British commander Baron Andrew Rollo sailed to Île Saint-Jean with four warships. His orders were to remove all the Acadians and to build a fort on the island. During Rollo's attack, the settlers fled. Rollo then destroyed all the

After the Seven Years' War, artists recreated the dramatic capture of Louisbourg and Île Royal in paintings.

Although it marked the end of their power in early Canada, the French celebrated the Treaty of Paris with a fireworks display in that city.

crops and killed the livestock to discourage the Acadians from returning.

British soldiers eventually caught most of the fleeing Acadians and shipped them to Louisbourg, which was now under British control. The Acadians were allowed to pack only their clothes, bedding, and some personal belongings. Dogs, horses, tools, dishes, and the rest of their possessions were left behind. From Louisbourg, the Acadians were loaded onto crowded ships and sent to France.

After the fall of Île Royale and Île Saint-Jean, the British continued attacking New France, the only remaining French colony in early Canada. Finally, in 1763,

the war came to an end. The French were defeated. In Europe, France and Great Britain signed the Treaty of Paris. According to the Treaty, France surrendered almost all of its land in North America to the British. New France became a British colony, and France's power in the region came to an end.

FURTHER UNDERSTANDING

The Treaty of Paris

The Treaty of Paris was signed on February 10, 1763, ending the Seven Years' War. It also put an end to France's empire in North America. The only territories that remained French were the islands of Saint-Pierre and Miquelon, off the coast of present-day Newfoundland and Labrador. French fishers were also allowed to land and dry their catch on the northern coast of Newfoundland and Labrador. Those French people who stayed in North America were allowed to remain Roman Catholic.

A New Acadia

Acadians thrived during the first half of the nineteenth century.

After the Seven Years' War, some Acadians were allowed to return to the Maritimes. Most of those who returned had escaped the initial deportation. Others had been prisoners of the British who were finally set free. Only a small number of the deported Acadians managed to make their way back to the Maritimes. All Acadians who returned to the Maritimes were required to pledge their loyalty to Great Britain.

Some returning Acadians founded small communities in Nova Scotia, Cape Breton Island, and Prince Edward Island. Most headed to eastern New Brunswick, a newly-created territory that had once been part of Nova Scotia. In all of these areas, British settlers occupied most of the land that formerly belonged to the Acadians. The remaining lands were too poor for agriculture, and the returning Acadians found themselves unable to farm. Instead, they turned to fishing and logging to make their living.

The resettled Acadians had few civil or political rights. Until 1763, they could not own land. Acadians were also not permitted to vote in some areas until 1810, and were not allowed to serve as members of the **legislature** until 1830.

Despite such discrimination, the Acadians thrived during the first half of the nineteenth century. In 1800, there were approximately 8500 Acadians in Nova Scotia, Prince Edward Island, and New Brunswick. By the late 1860s, their population had jumped to more than 87,000.

For the most part, the Acadians kept to themselves in their new settlements. There, they preserved their traditions, including cultural celebrations, food, language, music, and stories. Their isolation from the British allowed the Acadians to develop a unique culture in what would become Canada.

After the Seven Years' War, many Acadians travelled to Saint-Pierre and Miquelon, which still have Acadian populations today.

BECOMING CAJUN

Some deported Acadians eventually settled in Louisiana, a French colony in what is now the United States. There, they lived much as they had in early Canada. As Acadians mingled with other groups in Louisiana, a variation of Acadian culture developed. This culture was called "Cajun," from a mispronunciation of the word Acadian.

Approximately 1,000 Acadians settled in Louisiana between 1765 and 1768. The first families to arrive included the Blanchards, Poiriers, Giroirs, Guilbeaus, Moutons, and Savoies. Many had travelled by boat from Nova Scotia. Others had been sent to France before finding passage on ships headed for Louisiana. Some may have travelled by foot across the continent—what would have been a long and dangerous journey.

The Acadians settled along the Mississippi River on what came to be known as the Acadian Coast. The land there was fertile, and once again, the Acadians turned to farming. The fertile **bayou** lands of Louisiana allowed the newcomers to raise cattle and harvest corn, yams, sugarcane, and cotton.

The settlers maintained traditions brought from Acadia. Over time, these blended with traditions of other groups in the area to create Cajun culture. This culture is still present in the area today. Like Acadians in Canada, the Cajuns of Louisiana are known for their own unique cultural celebrations, food, folklore, language, music, and religious beliefs.

The Acadians settled on the Mississippi River on what came to be called the Acadian Coast.

The climate and landscape of the Mississippi River was a dramatic change for the Acadians from Atlantic Canada.

TIMELINE

Events of the past can be shown on timelines. This timeline shows the years 1000 through 1791.

1000
The Norse sail to North America for the first time.

1003
Thorvald Eriksson, a Norse explorer, encounters a group of Aboriginal Peoples in Canada.

1400
European merchants use overland routes to trade with Asia.

1440
New instruments and better maps help sailors find their way across oceans and seas.

1480
The search begins for a sea route to Asia. Some people sail east around Africa. Others sail west across the Atlantic.

1497
Explorer John Cabot reaches the Grand Banks near what is now Newfoundland.

1510
Fishers from Europe begin annual visits to the Grand Banks.

1520
Fishers begin to trade with Aboriginal Peoples along the eastern coast of North America.

1534
Explorer Jacques Cartier explores the Gulf of St. Lawrence and claims the area for the king of France.

1560
Hats made from beaver fur become fashionable in Europe.

1576
Explorer Martin Frobisher explores the coast of what is now Labrador and sails to Frobisher Bay by Baffin Island.

1605
The French start a settlement at Port-Royal. Explorer Samuel de Champlain begins a settlement at Quebec.

1610
Explorer Henry Hudson sails into Hudson Bay. The Huron help Champlain explore inland areas. French farmers settle in the St. Lawrence River valley.

1611

Jesuit missionaries come to Canada to teach Christian beliefs to the Aboriginal Peoples.

1639

Ursuline nuns come to Quebec.

1642

Ville-Marie is founded as a mission post on the island of Montreal.

1649

The Iroquois, Aboriginal allies of the British, wipe out the Huron, Aboriginal allies of the French, in a war for control of the fur trade.

1659

Radisson and Groseilliers explore the area northwest of the Great Lakes.

1670

The Hudson's Bay Company is formed by the British.

1691

Explorer Henry Kelsey reaches the Prairies and sees buffalo.

1713

The Treaty of Utrecht gives Great Britain control over part of eastern Canada and the land around Hudson Bay.

1731

Pierre Gaultier de Varennes et de la Vèrendrye begins exploring west of the Great Lakes and the Prairies.

1750

The British build a fortress at Halifax.

1755

The British expel the French settlers, called Acadians, from Nova Scotia.

1756

The Seven Years' War begins in Europe and spreads to North America.

1758

The French complete construction of Louisbourg, a fortress on Île Royale.

1760

The British destroy the French fortress at Louisbourg.

1763

The Treaty of Paris ends the Seven Years' War. Great Britain takes control of eastern Canada.

1774

The Quebec Act lets French settlers keep their language, religion, and some of their laws.

1783

The American colonies become the United States. Loyalist settlers from the United States move eastern Canada.

1791

The Constitutional Act divides Quebec into two provinces—Upper Canada and Lower Canada.

EXPULSION OF THE ACADIANS

Since the deportation of the Acadians from Canada in 1755, many people have accused Governor Charles Lawrence of behaving cruelly. Read this fictional debate to help you decide if the governor made a fair decision.

Michel: By 1755, most of the Acadians were born in North America. They promised to be neutral. They only wanted to live in peace and farm their land.

Betty: Why should Lawrence have believed the Acadians when they promised not to fight the British? When British soldiers captured Fort Beauséjour in 1755, there were 300 Acadians inside the fort. Some French priests encouraged the Mi'kmaq to fight the English.

Michel: In previous wars, the Acadians remained neutral. When France tried to convince them to move to Cape Breton or Prince Edward Island after the 1713 peace treaty, the Acadians refused to go.

Betty: But the Acadians would not sign the oath of allegiance.

Michel: Because the people who signed the oath could then be forced to fight for England against France. Acadians did not want to fight anyone.

Betty: There were more Acadians than English settlers, and this was British soil. It was a good strategy to deport them.

Michel: I disagree. The Acadians had been living on the land for more than a century before the English established their first settlement in Nova Scotia. I think Governor Lawrence made a cruel, unfair decision.

Reflecting on this issue ...

1. Why were the British concerned about the Acadians?
2. List the advantages and disadvantages of deporting the Acadians.
3. Suggest alternatives to deportation that the governor could have tried. How would these alternatives affect the Acadians and the British?
4. What would you have done if you had to make that decision? Work with a partner or in a small group.
5. Research to find out if Canadians today can remain neutral in time of war.

LOUISBOURG: RELIVING THE PAST

Events of the past can be brought to life through historical reconstructions. Reconstructions allow people to see restored artifacts being used and displayed in houses, forts, and other buildings from times past. People dressed in period clothing show visitors what living and working at the time was like.

Today, the fortress of Louisbourg on Cape Breton Island, Nova Scotia, is North America's largest historical reconstruction. The French began building the fortress in 1713. As many as 5,000 soldiers were stationed in its garrison at one time. Louisbourg changed hands several times before finally falling to the British in 1758.

The reconstruction of Louisbourg began in 1961. Restored buildings include the guardhouse, ice house, stables, governor's residence, carriage house, soldier's barracks, chapel, and prison.

Visitors to Louisbourg can see buildings and artifacts, as well as people in costumes performing different aspects of eighteenth-century life in the fort. The fortress' artifacts include the largest collection of eighteenth-century French furnishings outside of France. Cannons and piles of cannonballs still guard the thick stone walls, which echo with history. Evidence from surviving documents, artifacts, and ongoing archeological **excavations** has revealed much about the Acadians and life at Louisbourg.

On your own

1. Research some aspect of life at Louisbourg. Write a short report explaining what you have learned. Include any diagrams or drawings that you think might be necessary.
2. Write a diary entry from the point of view of someone living at Louisbourg, such as a soldier, fisher, government official, or servant.

In a small group

1. Visit a local museum or historical reconstruction to see how history can be brought to life.
2. Identify some objects in your home or school that may one day be used as artifacts by historians. Make a list of the different things each object would tell historians and archaeologists about life in the present.

FURTHER RESEARCH

How can I learn more about the Acadians?

Libraries

Most libraries have computers that connect to a database for searching for information. If you input a key word, you will be provided with a list of books in the library that contain information on that topic. Non-fiction books are arranged numerically, using their call number. Fiction books are organized alphabetically by the author's last name.

Internet Resources

The Internet can be an excellent source of information. For more reliable results, look for websites created by government agencies, non-profit organizations, and educational institutions. Online encyclopedias can also be a great source. Avoid personal web pages or sites that are trying to sell something.

Canada: A People's History Online

history.cbc.ca
The online companion to CBC's award-winning television series on the history of Canada, as told through the eyes of its people. This multimedia website features behind-the-scenes information, games and puzzles, and discussion boards. It is also available in French.

The Canadian Encyclopedia Online

www.thecanadianencyclopedia.com
A reference for all things Canadian. In-depth history articles are accompanied by photographs, paintings, and maps. Articles can be read in both French and English.

GLOSSARY

Algonquian: Aboriginal Peoples of the Eastern Subarctic

allies: people or nations who help each other

baptized: dipped in or washed with water as a sign of purification and admission to a Christian church

bayou: marshy land at the inlet or outlet of a lake, river, or gulf

cartographer: a map-maker

colonel: an mid-ranking officer in the British armed forces

colonists: people who have left their own country to settle in a new land

colony: a settlement created by people who have left their own country to settle in another land

deported: forced by authorities to leave one's home

documents: something written or printed that provides proof of a fact

excavations: the digging up of buildings or objects from the past

fur trade: an industry centred upon the trade of European goods for beaver furs from Aboriginal Peoples

garrison: soldiers stationed in a fort or town

Jesuit: a member of a religious group called the Society of Jesus

legislature: a group of people with the power to make laws for a province

looted: robbed

merchants: people who buy goods and sell them for higher prices

missionaries: members of religious orders who work to convert other people to their religion

monarchs: people who rule countries, such as queens and kings

mythology: traditional stories relating to a particular culture or person

neutral: taking neither side in a fight or an argument

nymphs: beautiful maidens with supernatual powers, who live in nature

peninsula: a piece of land almost surrounded by water

preserve: to keep from spoiling

Protestant: members of Christian churches that separated from the Roman Catholic church in Europe during the 1500s

resources: things that can be used to meet needs

Roman Catholic: the Christian church over which the Pope presides

supernatural: created or caused by a force outside the laws of nature; usually related to gods and spirits

treaty: a signed agreement between two or more countries

War of Spanish Succession: a war in Europe that lasted from 1701 to 1713 and involved the colonies in North America

INDEX